People of the Bible

The Bible through stories and pictures

Jonah
and the Whale

Jonah and the Whale, first published in the U.S.
by Raintree Publishers, Inc.
Copyright © 1983 in this format by Belitha Press Ltd.
Text copyright © 1983 by Catherine Storr
Illustrations copyright © 1983 by Barry Wilkinson

Published in 1988 by Ideals Publishing Corporation,
P.O. Box 148000, Nashville, Tennessee 37214-8000.
All rights reserved. No part of this book may be
reproduced in any form without permission in writing
from the publisher.
Printed and bound in the United States of America.

ISBN 0-8249-7305-4BK

Jonah
and the Whale

Retold by Catherine Storr
Pictures by Barry Wilkinson

IDEALS CHILDREN'S BOOKS

Nashville, Tennessee

There was once a man named Jonah, who lived near a seaport called Joppa. One day he heard God tell him, "Jonah! I want you to go to the great city of Nineveh. Tell the people there I am very angry with them. If they go on being so wicked, I shall punish them."

"Yes, God, I'll go," said Jonah. But he thought, "Why should I help these people? I won't go to Nineveh." Instead he went down to the harbor, and found a ship to take him to another city, called Tarshish. He bought his ticket and went on board the ship.

"Aha!" he thought, "God won't know where I have gone."

But he was wrong. God did know where he was, and sent a great storm after the ship. The wind blew hard. The waves were enormous.

The sailors were terrified. "The ship will sink and we shall drown," they thought. So they threw some of the cargo over the side to make the ship lighter.

Jonah did not hear the storm. He was in his cabin asleep.

The captain of the ship woke him up. "What are you doing," he said, "sleeping through this terrible storm? Get up and pray to God. Ask him to stop the wind from blowing so hard, or else we are all going to die."

The sailors said, "God must be angry with someone who is on this ship, and that is why we are all in danger. Let's draw lots to find out who it is."

Jonah was the unlucky man.

"Where do you come from?" the sailors asked him. "Is God punishing you for something wicked you have done?"

"I am a Jew," said Jonah, "and my God is the God of heaven, who made both the sea and the land. He told me to go to Nineveh, but I didn't want to. I came on this ship so that I could go to Tarshish instead. You had better throw me into the waves. Then God will let you sail away on a calm sea."

The sailors did not want to throw Jonah
into the sea. They rowed hard, trying to get
the ship safely to land.

But at last they saw that they would never
be able to do this, so they threw Jonah into
the huge waves.

As Jonah fell down the side of the ship, the wind dropped. The waves became calmer. The ship sailed safely on its way, and Jonah fell into the deep sea. He found himself going into the mouth of an enormous whale. The whale gulped. Jonah went straight down into its belly.

Jonah was very frightened. He prayed to God from inside the whale's belly. "Please, God, listen to me! I prayed to you before and you saved me. This time you have sent me down to the bottom of the sea. The huge waves rolled over me, and seaweed wrapped itself around my head. I nearly died. Then I remembered that if I asked you, you could save me from this danger, too."

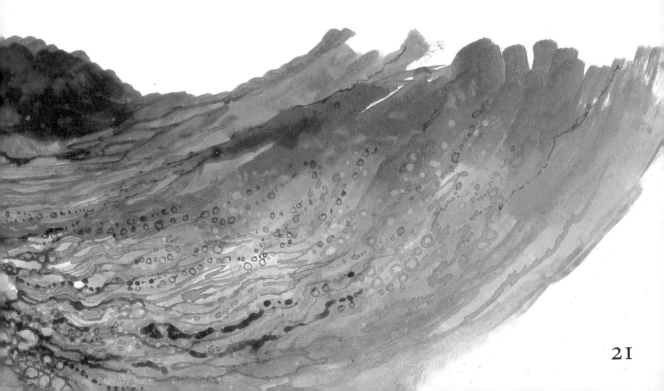

God listened to him, and he said to the
whale, "Spew Jonah up out of your belly
and see that he comes out of your mouth
onto dry land."

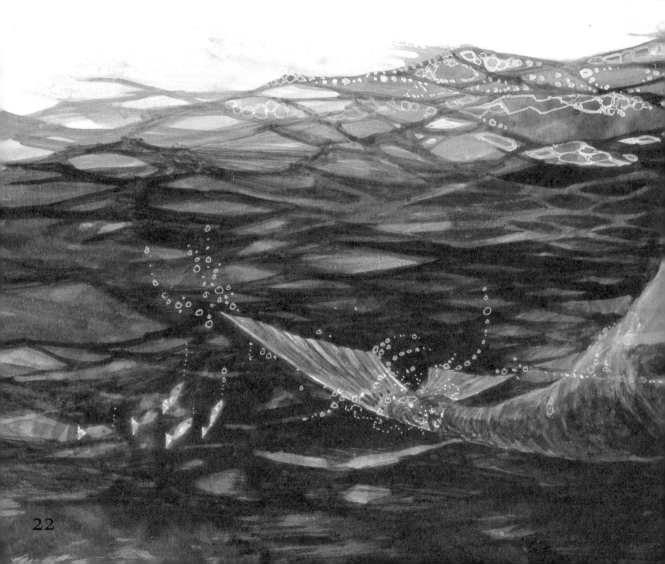

The whale heard what God said, and he
spewed Jonah up onto a beach.

Then God told him again that he must go
to Nineveh. This time Jonah knew he had to
do what he was told, even though it would
take him three days to travel to Nineveh.

When he arrived, Jonah told the people of Nineveh what had happened to him. "I have come to warn you," he said, "that God will punish you if you go on being wicked."

The King of Nineveh heard Jonah's warnings and was frightened. He took off his grand clothes and put on a robe made of sackcloth.

He told his people, "You must wear sackcloth and sit in ashes, like me. We must stop eating and drinking so much. We must tell God we are sorry."

"Do not feed your animals," the king said. "Put sackcloth on them as well, and tell God that you are sorry."

When God saw that the people of Nineveh were sorry, he did not punish them.

Bible Lands of the Old Testament

Mt. Ararat

Tarshish

R. Tigris

R. Euphrates

Nineveh

Mediterranean Sea

Nazareth

Sea of Galilee

Joppa

Jerusalem

Bethlehem

Hebron

Canaan

Sodom

Land of Goshen

Babylon

Succoth

Memphis

SINAI

Ur of the Chaldees

EGYPT

Thebes